MESSAGE OF CONCERN

Removal of All Images That Attempt To Portray Divine

Imam W. Deen Mohammed®

ISBN- 978-1481968188

CONTENTS

ACKNOWLEDGMENTS   4

ABBREVIATIONS CLARIFIED   6

MESSAGE OF CONCERN   7

ABOUT THE AUTHOR   93

Imam W. Deen Mohammed, *leader of the largest community of Muslims in the United States of America passed on September 9, 2008. We pray that his work continues to grow and serve humanity as he would have desired it to, through all of us who have benefited so greatly from his teachings. Ameen*

Structure, Guard And Publish The Knowledge

"We need knowledge, then we need protection for it. How do you protect knowledge? Some people say, "You protect knowledge by not letting anybody interfere with it. Don't let anybody change it. Publish it! When you publish it, people know it. That's its protection." Yes! If you want to protect your knowledge, publish it! When you publish it, it is protected and the people know it. But if you keep it locked up to yourself, you will die and your knowledge will die with you. Or your enemy will get a hold to it and he will publish it after you in a corrupt form.

Thus, Allah (swt) says. "And We have revealed it for the express purpose that it should be propagated." Yes! That is its guarantee that it will be protected. When it's propagated in its right form, then the people will inherit it directly. They don't have to listen to what you have to say. You won't have to tell them what Prophet Muhammad (pbuh) said, they got it directly. It was published by him in his lifetime.

If we want to guard the knowledge that we have, we must publish it. The more people know about it, the more it is guaranteed that it will live and it won't be changed. The less people know about it, the better the chance that it will die with us, or be changed. Yes! We structure the knowledge and we propagate the knowledge." *Imam W. Deen Mohammed*

Abbreviations Clarified

G-d for God
In this book the word God is written as G-d for the respect of the word "god" because some people mirror to disrespect it with the word "dog".

SWT for Subhana Wa Tallah
The abbreviation after Allah (SWT) means "Subhana Wa Tallah" in Arabic which means "The Sacred and The Mighty" in English.

PBUH for Peace Be Upon Him
The abbreviation after Prophet Muhammad (PBUH) means "May the Peace and Blessings of Allah (G-d) be upon him" in English and "Sal Allahu Allahi Wa Salam" in Arabic.

AS for Alayhi Salam
The abbreviation (AS) means "Alayhi Salam" in Arabic, which means "May Allah (G-d) bless him" in English.

MESSAGE OF CONCERN

*Dallas, TX August 21, 1982 at the C.R.A.I.D. meeting
Committee For The Removal Of All Images That
Attempt To Portray Divine*

The Final Step

As Salaam Alaikum Bismillah Ir-Rahman – Ir- Rahim

Praise be to Allah. Muslims, People, Friends. Peace be unto you. As we say in our Language. As – Salaam – Alaikum.

I am before you to address the need for the **removal of images in religion** that invite the members of the religions to worship, or to address those images as Deities, or as G-d's.

First, let me express a belief that is in scripture, and it is a kind of general principal, but it says something that I think will help us understand our problems, and it may be a good start for this address. We read in the Bible these words, "A tree is known by the fruit it bears." Regarding these images in religion, especially the Crucifix, I believe that what I am about to mention to you, is a product of that tree.

There's now a movement, headed by a man who was once a member in the Nation of Islam, officially called in those days (the lost found Nation of Islam in the Wilderness of North America) . There's is a man who now heads a religious organization, or religion, (in fact he heads the religion), he has formed his own religion, and he has also formed his own bible. His bible is called (the black bible). It's not a cheap effort. He spent some money to put it together, and to have it printed. The pictures you will find in that bible, are mostly pictures of black people, and Satan in that bible is pictured, or depicted as a white man. The scene of Adam and Eve in the garden shows Adam and Eve, Black, and the serpent, (presenting the picture of the Devil), is the white man. This is, without any question, Black reaction in religion, to White Man's Image, in religion. If that's one of the fruits of the Crucifix, then we have to acknowledge as right minded sensible people, that that is a bad Fruit.

We hope to establish our reasons for insisting upon the removal of all images in religion, and that is our first reason. That it produces reactions in the conscience of people, that don't identify racially with the image, that are bad for society, and that represents only the furtherance of that kind of confusion and corruption. We're not attacking Christianity. We respect Christianity with sacred respect. We're not attacking Jesus, (peace be upon him). We respect Jesus Christ with Sacred respect. Let us continue.

And now, I would like to go to the positive side of the Crucifix. That is to say, that it has its good influence as well. And we as intelligent people should be able to weigh its good influence, or its good utility, with its bad influences, (if you agree with us), and its harmful utility, and make a decision, as to whether it is acceptable to leave the Image in society, or to remove it.

Another reason we have for insisting upon the removal of all Images in religion is that, the Crucifix, while it is true, that it does have some benefit, in terms of the kind of catharsis, or the kind of purging of wrong mindedness, on the part of people, that it offers, or that it holds. It has some benefits. When we look at a human being, or a human form, pitifully nailed to a cross, and we're told that person was a good person; that person had no malice, no ill will; that person was well-natured, and meant well to everybody, it does draw our sympathies toward him. And when our sympathies are drawn toward a good thing, it does have the effect of awakening our good nature, and our good conscience. So that's a good side of it. But in spite of it having that kind of influence, to provoke the movement or stir of good sentiments, moral sentiments, compassion etc., in the one who looks upon it. For Races that cannot identify with it racially, it has a reverse effect. It has a very negative effect. And not only for races that can't identify with it. Even for those who identify with it simply because it's in their Image, it has a reverse effect, it has a negative effect.

Now people. There is an understanding in Psychology, that the Human Conscious can be transported, and detached, and lose all identity with the concern that it previously belonged to, if you can transfer that particular consciousness, and its concerns to an Image.

In very early times of man's cultural growth or evolution, the psychologist, or the psychiatrist, and the priest were all in one person. He was the magic worker, or the witch doctor as we call him now, (he took on a bad name when the sciences evolved). And the witch doctor, he would form an Image, and He would use that Image to drum up emotions, sentiments and emotions, and draw those sentiments and emotions to the Image, until the person became almost spellbound. In fact many of the people He was treating, would fall out. They would lose consciousness and they would fall out. Some would go into fits. But after the experience was over, most of His patients felt better, because He had detached their own consciousness from the subject of that consciousness, from the owner of that consciousness. He had detached their own concerns, from the owner of those concerns, and he had made it possible for them to experience their own existence in the Image, rather than in themselves.

And I tell you with scientific proof. I tell you that's what has happened to many non-Caucasian people all over the world, where that Image has been established, where that Image has been accepted, of a white man or of a European looking man, or of a European Jewish looking man, on a cross. They have been successful. Who am I talking about? I'm talking about people who saw this utility in the Crucifix.

People who didn't mean well. People who wanted to capture the productive forces of other people for their own selfish purposes. People who wanted to empty out the concerns for the individual's life, and attach it to an Image, so that they could drive those individuals to inhuman extremes, to inhuman conditions. Suppress them with inhuman circumstances, inhuman burdens, and they would find it possible to survive, and be happy all the time, everyday, because their reality was no longer in themselves, Their reality was in the Image.

Now, let me see if I can explain this in a different way. You know you can experience a thing factually, and you can experience a thing through the medium of fantasy. You can experience a thing factually, and you can experience a thing vicariously, By vicariously we mean that you have become so absorbed in the thing that you're beholding, that you experience now what that thing is experiencing. So I can be enjoying music, and you can become so absorbed in watching me enjoy music that you become me. And now, you're enjoying music, just as I'm enjoying music. And you're enjoying the music through me. And your situation is not my situation. I'm free to enjoy the music. They have you handcuffed. They have your feet shackled. They have your mouth muzzled, but you see me, and you're doing the same thing I'm doing, with your hands shackled, your feet shackled, your mouth muzzled, but you're doing the same thing I'm doing. In your soul inside, you're bouncing with me. You're doing everything I'm doing, But you're not doing it factually, you're doing it vicariously.

Now, let us go on to explain what we're talking about. So in psychology, this is called transference, where the persons own reality has been transferred to something else. Now, suffering people will identify with a suffering image, or with an Image that represents the sufferer. It's easy to get them, suffering, to identify with the Image that represents the sufferer. So, no matter what color he is, no matter what ethnic image he has, if you see suffering, the human being is more a spiritual creature than he is a physical creature.

So, if they can show you, that spiritually, you are the same. He is a spiritual sufferer. You are a spiritual sufferer. His free spirit is oppressed, yours too. He has been wronged in the world, You too. He has been denied the freedom of movement – His hands are nailed, yours too. He has been denied the freedom of progress – His feet are nailed, yours too. He has had his heart injured, his heart is bleeding, but he can't do anything about it. Yours too.

If they can make a picture that identifies very closely with your own reality, then it's easy to transfer your reality to that image, and then you can stay in the dung house, you can stay

14

in the dungeon, you can stay in ignorance, and you can find satisfaction through the image. Now, excuse my language. Occasionally I will say, dung; excuse my language. Now, if we have been able to come that far, and see what we are talking about, and understand what we're talking about, I say we're on the way to removing these images.

Because once any intelligent minded, free thinking person sees this reality, He has to commit himself for life, to get rid of that image. We're still on the second reason.

The second reason is a psychological reason. The second reason is, this thing that it docs to our psychology, that robs us of attachment with our own reality. Now if I'm correct, won't this explain the lack of motivation in the black man. The lack of community aggressiveness on the part of the black community. Won't this explain the lack of stability on the part of the black community, and won't this also explain the divisions, and the lack of unity on the part of the black community, and not only on the part of the black community, but on the part of the Hispanic community, and on the part of every other community that hasn't been able to identify with the image, in its ethnicity, in its physical reality.

Now, let's look at what kinds of messages come from that image to the white man. To the white man, he sees a sufferer too, and if he's suffering, he identifies with the suffering Jesus also, but he has something that you don't have.

He knows that that Jesus is also called lord, and you know that you aren't a lord. And he knows that in the worlds situation that he lives in, the white man is boss, and that white image on the cross is called lord, so in his subconscious, or through his conscience, he is satisfied with that identity in a way that you could never be satisfied.

You're satisfied with it because he was a good man, and he suffered too, but G-d redeemed him and took him up into heaven, so you find satisfaction in that hope, that 'I too', because I now have become like that image on the cross. I too have hope. The lord that redeemed the image, will redeem me one day, and I too will have a place of glory and dignity in the after-world.

The Muslim challenged that idea. Because our Holy Book says, "Get with all the means that you have at your

fingertips. Work for the afterlife, the afterworld, But don't forget your share in this world." That's what our Holy Book says.

So it's not enough for a Muslim. If a Muslim who knows his religion, he won't be able to accept the message of the cross, because he can't wait for the here-after to get his due respect, his due recognition, his due share in the possessions and in the authority of this one, and that he knows that G-d has obligated him to earn his ticket into the next, on the strength of what He has done.

And if he hasn't done much for a share in the controls of material things on this earth, then he hasn't earned much as a ticket into the next world. In our religion, mind you. Now I'm not saying that in Christianity this idea doesn't exist, but for the majority of Christians, this idea doesn't exist. There are only a very few Christians who also put that heavy emphasis on getting a descent share in this world, that's required too. But, we'll come to that point later.

The Constitution of these United States respect that as a sacred concern, and a sacred need in man. We'll come to that later. We're still on the second point. Now dear people, that Caucasian, or white person, or person that sees a close and striking resemblance between them, and the image on the cross, has an advantage that those who can't identify with it that way, are lacking; don't have. And again, I repeat, that advantage is the identity with the Lord. The identity with the Superior Being. The identity with the Judge. Jesus will also sit in judgment. Is that right? So they have identity with the owner.

Say! 'O yes, G-d gave Jesus Christ everything, and the white man says yes, we have got everything. And G-d gave Jesus Christ authority. And the white man says yes, we have got authority. And G-d made Jesus Boss, or Jesus Lord. And the white man will say, Yes, we are boss.

But when you look at it, no such ideas can come in your mind, because your reality does not agree with that part of the image. So, isn't this an injustice.

If this image is going to be an image for all the people. If this is an image for all races, isn't that an injustice? So here and now, we establish the second reason for the removal for that image.

Now, let us go on to the third one. The third reason that we will establish today for the removal of that Image is the conflict that Image hold for the Life of the American people, and I'm talking about the national life, the political life of the American people, as that life is understood, or interpreted by the Constitution of these United States.

The Constitution of these United States established that man has one nature. And that all men have same potential for growth and that all men are entitled to ownership, freedom, or the ownership of material possessions, political freedom, the right to aspire to the highest office of these United States, along with every other man, or every other citizen.

This is the concept in the Constitution of These United States of America. The Constitution of the United States recognize the sacred dignity of the human person. It does not give priority to ethnicity over what is essentially, the human being.

And as a consequence of that particular recognition being in the Constitution of the United States, and in the life of the American People, we have found that the movement of freedom and justice have trampled down ethnic concerns to establish the human concerns and to do justice by it.

We have no problem with the Constitution of the United States, but - The Crucifix itself, is in direct conflict with the spirit of that Constitution, when it holds up the picture of one race and calls Lord! In the face of the fact that white man, pretending to be a Scientist within the last one hundred years, falsely established that Black people are racially inferior to white. That the white man and the black man are not of the same substance.

They are not on the same level in the social evolution, the **Cultural Evolution of Man**. That the black man has been fixed by divine decree, into a lower level of social and cultural evolution, and that the white man has to always be the guardian of the black man. This is what they established in their so called Sciences, not too long ago. This is History.

In the face of that now, how can they dare tolerate the lifting of a white image, or a Caucasian image, as a deity, as a G-d, as an Image of G-d's son, in whom G-d manifests. No wonder all the faith we have in religion is spiritual faith. No wonder we get no place in religion, other than an emotional bang bang. It's because, that Image say's that G-d chose a white man as a medium for His expression. Not a black man, a white man, for the medium of His expression.

Some of you will say, "well man, it could have been anybody. It could have been a black one". And if it would have been a black one, the white man would have been in our situation after a few centuries. So we don't accept that. And some will say, "well, what about your Prophet Mohammed?". Was He a Negro? Yes! "Was He an African? No! By the white man's classification, a Negro is anybody with any amount of African Blood in his veins. And according to the history of our Prophet (PBUH), he had African Blood, and Caucasian Blood in His Veins, and the two of them met and made Arab. Now, that's not admissible. I only said that for emotional effect. That's not even admissible in this discussion. The point is this. Here is the

point. Mohammed was not a G-d. He established that He was not a god.

He established that he was a human being, just like us. In fact, the Sacred Scripture that he delivered, It says in The Sacred words of G-d in the Qur,an, "Tell them Mohammed. I am a mortal just like you". Now it didn't leave any doubt, didn't leave any question. It didn't say, I'm a mortal and stop there, because some would say, "yes he was a mortal with the Divine Life in him". It says, "tell them O-Mohammed, I am a mortal just like you."

In answer to what was corrupted in the New Testament, where Jesus said, "I in you, and you in me". Saying that we are One Nature. We are of the same Essence. Whatever has sparked in me, the possibility exists also for you.

Now, let me say again. The Qur'an is not a white picture book, in fact it has no pictures at all. Not even our Prophet. We don't have a picture of our Prophet. There is no picture of him existing. G-d directed him to outlaw any imagery of that kind.

Now, let me proceed. And understand now, that He himself, came in the movement of truth that was before Him. He came into it by G-d's will to complete it. So whatever He established, it has its justification in the Prophets that were behind Him. Now, let me proceed a little further with this. Another point is that the Qur'an, (Our Holy Book), says, there never existed any race on this earth that G-d did not raise up from among them a Prophet. So, our book doesn't make Prophet-hood a white concern, or a white dignity.

Our Book makes Prophet-hood, the dignity of all people. And our Book goes on to say that there are Prophets named in this scripture, and others that are not named, and it says also, and I repeat it again, that never was there a community of people that did not have a Prophet. All the communities behind Prophet Mohammed (pbuh) had Prophet's.

All the nations, all the races had their Prophet's. It is generally believed among Muslims presently on this earth, and it has been believed for a long time that the Prophet called Luqman, (The Wise, in the Qur'an), was a Black African. So we think we can go on now that we have pointed to that kind of wrong, and injustice, we can go on now and finish that point, and go on to our final point, the final point, in this address.

The Science Of The Crucifix

We see in the science of the Crucifix; and it's a Science because it touches the human psychology in an effort to preserve human morality, so it's a Science. We see in this science, a step in the long progression of society's effort to preserve morality for the individual, and for society. We know that when the moral concern leaves society, the society is thrown into confusion, chaos, and pretty soon there's social turmoil, destruction, and abuses of human rights. Tyrant's come into being. Tyrant's come into position, and dominate the good life of the people.

One great philosopher, western philosopher too, (I can't recall his name just now). He says that political leaders don't determine the future of society, or the future of a people.

It's the moral content of that society that determines it's future, because, once the moral content of that society is muffled or corrupted, or destroyed, the people will be

open for the tyrant to fish in the waters of their sensitivities, and throw bait out to them that will enslave them.

And how many of us have grabbed the promise of more money, and gave our allegiance to a tyrant. How many of us have grabbed the promise of more life and more sex, and more freedom for our lust, and accepted the tyrant. In fact, many of us who go to the polls, we go there for moral reasons.

We choose a man because he will license our weaknesses, and not bear down on our weaknesses to bring strength. So we choose him. We choose the weak leader that will allow us to keep on going with our weaknesses. Is that right? Yes! We know this to be a fact. So, when the moral content leaves the society, the fate of that society is in the hand of the biggest criminal that can come up, or the biggest beast, that can rise on the land. Whoever can wield the biggest stick of authority will take over the life of that people. But people will die. They will lose their life. They will even sacrifice their wife and their husbands. They will even sacrifice their children for a moral principal that they have been converted upon, or a moral principal that they think is crucial to the whole life of the people. Yes! They will die.

So moral concerns make men martyrs, and a tyrant can't deal with people like that. And what we are saying here that the Crucifix that is purposely designed to stimulate consciousness in people that look on it and in that kind of activity, preserve the moral life for them or for society, has so many other negative, kinds of influences coming from it, that it doesn't justify us even keeping it for that utility.

Before going to the final concern, I want to talk to you more on this one, because it needs much more talk, and we don't have time, because we put ourselves on time today and I'm going to have to complete it. But, let us look at the symbolism now... symbolism... symbolism. Isn't the Cross a symbol.

Now, if Jesus Christ went up in heaven whole soul and body, then I know, (maybe you don't), but I know that his Body, too, was a symbol. How come I know that? I know that because the Bible says "flesh cannot enter the kingdom". All right! That's how I know it. I know that the Bible say's flesh

cannot enter the kingdom. So I have to look for an interpretation now.

They say "Jesus (pbuh) went to heaven whole soul and body". Now I have to look for an interpretation, because the Bible say's, (and doesn't apologize for it), flesh cannot enter the kingdom. So then, Jesus' body must also be a symbol. So we have one symbol Crucified upon another symbol. Is that right (if you follow me)? If you follow me, then one symbol has been Crucified upon another symbol. And you know, if you take one symbol that's a Cross, and then you take another symbol, and you make it a Cross, and you Crucify it on that Cross, 'That's a Double Cross'. Now, let's see what has been Double Crossed. For Jesus is a symbol now in his flesh and a symbol in the Cross, so let's see now what is the Double Cross.

In the Beginning, there was the word, and the word took on flesh, and dwelled with men. So the word has been Double Crossed. The word of truth has been Double Crossed, and Jesus (pbuh) is only a symbol of that word that has been Double Crossed. I mean Jesus (pbuh) in his Crucifix presentation, in the Crucifix form. It's only a symbol of the word, 'Double Cross.

How can we ever come to the understanding of the word, if they're going to keep in our eyes, keep us spellbound, enchanted and spellbound while we behold the white man on a Cross (in flesh). We have reduced this down now to manageable reality. We're no more in the mystery now, we can deal with this reality. We're talking about the word of truth.

Now, we're going to kind of digress a bit, and look at the growth of imagery outside of that limited context. We find that imagery has occupied man since time. Immemorial, we cannot recall exactly when this kind of thing came into being, that man, for as far as we can trace back, have grasped symbols that held the meanings for them because they identified in that symbol their idea, or concept, or whatever, so man has had to struggle for expression. He gets an idea. He gets a feeling. He gets an emotion. He has an experience, an internal experience, and He wants to communicate it. He finds himself without the ability to communicate what he's experiencing. And Allah has taught him through what medium? Allah has taught him to communicate through the medium of the external reality. And the oldest living example we have of this kind of progression, or evolution of man's effort to communicate, is in the Ancient Egyptian language they call Hieroglyphics.

Hieroglyphics is a picture language. It's a language of concrete concepts.

We have dogs there, we have suns there. We have daylight. We have fire. We have birds. We have wolves. We have all of these images put together to make a script. They put images together, and they made a script. And in order to read that script, you had to read their images. And it became good to them. See, the primitive man has come into that naturally. We find un-evolved, I hate to say primitive, but we find un-evolved society's all over the world, that speak in concretes.

They haven't learned how to speak in abstracts. So they speak in concrete pictures. But, we don't find any as evolved, and established as that language of Ancient Egypt. They have a mystery associated with this particular thing in Ancient Egypt, and this mystery is told in this way.

It says that 'When anybody came into the capital of Ancient Egypt, they had to first break the riddle before they could enter'. If they couldn't break the riddle of the muse, (now you know muse, if you want to understand it, muse means something that holds prophecy, something that can give you divine guidance. That's what it meant in ancient times). But, you know now, muse has become Amusement. And I even believe then, for the foolish, it was amusement, but for the wise, it was direction. And they would come up to the city, and they would behold the muse, which was a great statue. It too was an image. It was a huge statue, and it was imposing and mysterious.

So, it would captivate you. You know it would just suck you into it. And if you couldn't break the riddle, you couldn't get into that city. Not that you couldn't get into that city, (you could go physically into that city), but you couldn't make progress in that city.

Now, we are physically in America, but for now, after three generations, after three centuries, and many generations, we have not progressed.

"Yes we have. What about Andrew Young!" Ask Andrew Young what about his situation. Talk to him now, please. Go talk to Mayor Andrew Young, the former Ambassador of the United States, and if he doesn't depress you, come back to me baby, and I will apologize. We had men in stately places during Reconstruction. In fact, we had more significant positions in the political structure during Reconstruction then we have had since Reconstruction. So that's no proof of our advancement.

The proof of our advancement is our ability to command our own wards. Now I don't know what you call it here in this area, but in Chicago we have precincts, districts, and wards. And so far we haven't been able to command a district. We haven't been able to command a ward. We haven't been able to command a precinct. Our precinct captain, he relates between us and the city, or City Hall for their advantages. We see them getting advantages from us, but so far, our realities, our political realities, our economic realities, our business, material realities stay the same.

We are not stable communities. We don't have an equal share in the authority over our area. We don't have equal representation in the capitol, or in the material resources of the area. We are in fact, in the same situations, considering how everything else has progressed, how everything else has advanced. We are in the same situations that we were in when the man said, "go, we're going to give you forty acres and a mule" but did not fulfill his promise. Now, I know some of you will say, "Oh, brother Imam, please don't talk like that. We are Americans. We are American Muslim Mission."

That's right. And the Mission is to make America deliver. Yes, Yes, don't forget. That's part of the Mission. We have to make America deliver. And to do that, we're going to have to have some kind of possession of our own realities, and we have to begin with our personal self.

And anytime your whole conscience, and all your concerns can be transferred to an Image that you cannot identify ethnically with because it's an ethnic image, buddy, that tells me that we have to do something about getting control and possession of our own reality's. Yes, let us continue.

So, Ancient Egypt had a riddle. And the key for entering that city, (entering that city means becoming a part of that city, a functional part of that city, a progressive unit in that city). That's what it means by entering the city. Now we know those people that scripture say were in bondage, or enslaved by Pharaoh, the Lord of Egypt, who himself claimed very much what they claimed for the Crucifix. He claimed that He was the Lord of the Earth. In fact, He said that He was Lord of Everything. And He claimed his on the same ground's. He said, "The heavenly G-d had Chosen Him, and His Descendents, as an Earthly Embodiment for their Presence, or for His Presence, The Heavenly Lord's Presence). And Pharaoh, when He was questioned about Him saying that He was G-d, He said "Well, no, I'm not G-d in that sense, I am G-d Manifest, G-d is in Me".

And when the Prophet in our Scripture challenged Pharaoh, Pharaoh said, "I know no Lord but Me". Yes, that's what Pharaoh said. And do you know they had one of the most elaborate religious orders that history have recorded. We're not talking about savage man. We're not talking about barbaric man. We're talking about an Ancient Kingdom that

knew Science, knew Medicine, knew Chemistry, knew Physics. We're talking about an ancient kingdom about three, four, five thousand years ago, that made the first dust pan, that made the first broom to sweep the trash up, that made the first modern furniture.

Some of your modern furniture today, does not look any more modern than the furniture they have in the museum of Cairo Egypt that those people made three and four thousand years ago. And I'm speaking from firsthand knowledge. I saw this myself. Oh, we're not talking about a shabby society, a shabby nation. We're talking about an advanced, well established nation. A nation that boasted in its material accomplishments. In its Industry. A nation that boasted in its Sciences.

Getting Into Egypt Is Breaking The Riddle

A nation from which we trace our own science we call psychology. And you who have studied psychology, you know this. That's if you have studied it. If you have been trained in it by the white man, maybe you don't know it. But if you have done a little research on your own you know this.

If you have thought enough about the field, you're interested in to trace its beginnings in History, you have traced its beginnings back to Africa, to Ancient Egypt. Now, the people who were in bondage in Egypt, their main hope was to free themselves from Egypt. Now they were in Egypt weren't they. Now the one who wanted to come in, He had to do what? Break the riddle. Now, according to the Bible, the Hebrew children were already in Egypt. So what does this tell us? If they were in bondage, they didn't break the riddle. And if they were in bondage, they hadn't gotten into Egypt. Now, haven't our struggles as minority people been to get into the mainstream of America's life. Now we know we have been all the time haven't we. But we haven't been in the mainstream of America's life.

During reconstruction we had men in high places of government, but we haven't, we were not yet able to get into the mainstream of the American life. And since then, we've had men become rich. We can point to individual black men, individual black women, and say, oh, millionaires, multimillionaires, but still we're trying to get into the mainstream of America's life. Now look back there at that time. Didn't they have their Dathan. Wasn't Dathan sitting on a couch of luxury, and He was one of the Hebrew children. Yeah, Dathan was one of the Hebrew boys. And in Egypt, He sat on a couch of luxury. In the movie about the Hebrews, he had so many fine jewelry, rings and things on his hand, until it looked like luxury was a curse on him but, he was happy as he could be. And I think it was Edward G. Robinson, yes, he played Dathan. Yes, he was the Hebrew that was well off, but the Hebrew's were in bondage.

Now, I'm trying to tell you to look at this reality, and see yourself. We have a Muhammad Ali. We have a Johnson's Products Company. We have a few well to do heavy pocket Bilalians. But the state of the Bilalian at large is the state of the Hebrew boy's in bondage. We are not yet in Egypt. And getting into Egypt is not getting money in your pocket. Getting into Egypt is breaking the riddle. Oh, you heard that old expression, "a fool and his money soon parts". And that's the sad story of our people in the world. A fool and his money soon part.

So, let me move on up a little bit with this now. Now, remember, we're just on the third. We have one more to go. We haven't yet finished the third one. We wanted to show you the symbolism associated with this problem. Now, what happened now. The Hebrews, with the help of G-d. They had to have Allah. They couldn't make it without Allah. With the help of Allah, their uneducated man, Moses. How do we know he was uneducated? Maybe he was an intelligent man. In fact I'm convinced he was a very intelligent man, but he didn't have the scholarly ability of the Egyptian Leaders.

The proof of it, is that He said, "Oh G-d, untie the knot in my tongue". And since he couldn't speak very well, He asked G-d, he said, "appoint my brother Aaron, and make him a representative for me." Obviously, Aaron was articulate; obviously Aaron was erudite, (means learned), yes, obviously he had been on academic errands, and had become wise. Aaron, that is.

But he didn't have the conviction that his brother Moses had. He was still attached to the crumbs that fell off the table of Pharaoh. He still had his heart in that. He belonged to the religious community. He was the religious head, but he wasn't grounded in what Moses had been established in by G-d.

The proof of it is, G-d told him, "now don't you let Aaron get into this. Now that's your business. I'm charging you with this. You let Aaron speak, but you do the acting". So, Moses, he was given the responsibility of leading the movement. Taking the people out of bondage into freedom, and he needed Aaron for appropriate expression when he wanted to talk to the educated. So when he went back to Pharaoh, Aaron spoke for him, right? G-d communicated to Moses, and Moses transported that, or communicated that to Aaron, and Aaron articulated it before Pharaoh and his learned people.

We have the same situation today. We have the learned, who are very articulate, but they don't see the strategy in the cultural and social pattern. They don't see the strategy. They can't break the riddle, so they can't be charters of progress into freedom out of Egypt. You need someone else for that. And again, G-d has chosen the one who have difficulty with his tongue. He does not have a degree. He's not polished. He hasn't been on the errands of academia. So you know, he's at a disadvantage. So, I would like to talk to President Reagan. But I don't know if I can do it. Now this was your

leader five years ago. But G-d fulfilled his promise to Moses. He has taken the knot out of his tongue.

Now, didn't Moses pray for G-d to take the knot out of his tongue. And he asked G-d for a helper to articulate for him, didn't he? And the scripture never tells you that Moses became articulate. But it leaves that for the imagination of the religious scholars. For them to discover, that yes, he only used Aaron when he was in that situation. But later on, at the mountain, he saw into the riddles.

He saw into the symbols and he came down and Aaron didn't speak for him, did he? Instead, he spoke to Aaron, didn't he? He said, Aaron, what's the matter with you. You're the last one I thought would get hung up in these riddles. Now, what are you doing taking the ear rings of these people and smelting them down and making a golden calf. You should know better Aaron." And Aaron backed up in fright and fear. He said, please don't grab my beard. Don't grab me by the hair of my head. So look, we're trying to get to a point. We're trying to complete our third point.

And the spirit of G-d is on us and I can't stop. I'm trying to complete a third point. Now, let us look. When he got out of Egypt, he went out of, we would say, "the pot, into the frying pan". When he was in Egypt, Pharaoh was the threat.

But when he got out there in the wilderness, His own people threatened him. And out there in the wilderness they didn't have the conveniences of Cairo Egypt. Those conveniences were not out there. So his people began to mumble and grumble saying, "Yeah, you are our leader. you say you're G-d sent. Yeah, you've taken us out of one situation to put us into a worst. Say, at least in Egypt we could eat collard greens, black eyed peas, ham hocks, onions, lentils, and all kinds of pot herbs. But out here Moses, you've got us eating nothing. We can't live off this single kind of stuff here you're feeding us. You've got one kind of food out here. And another thing. When we were in Egypt, we had more money. Even though we were in bondage, we had more money. But out here we aren't got no money, we aren't got decent food. We're just lost in the wilderness".

And Moses said, I got a word from G-d, for that disrespectful, ungraceful kind of talk on your part. Do you recall the miracles that brought you here? Do you recall the great wonders that made it possible for you to get out of Egypt without them slaying all of us? So G-d, because of this terrible disrespect and ingratitude on your part, is going to make you wander out here for forty years.

Oh please tell him, "excuse us please." Tell your Lord to forgive us, we can't stay out here no forty years. He said, yeah, I know that. All you hypocrites are going to die during the forty years and when you die off, then G-d will give the Kingdom to a new people. That was their punishment for ingratitude.

So, let us see what happened in the Wilderness. This particular problem he had with his people, you know, the problem He had in Egypt, it was dealt with, with a stick wasn't it? G-d said, "that stick you got in your hand Moses, I'm going to let you in to some secrets that's are that stick". And when G-d showed him the first sign of the secrets that was in that stick, Moses got frightened, and jumped back from it. G-d said, "don't be afraid". He said, "approach it".

It had turned into a serpent, moving like a poison Cobra. G-d said," now grab it up in your hand". And when Moses grabbed it, the thing stretched back out and became a stick again. So Moses had faith. He said, "Oh, this is the Lord." He said, "Oh, I'm ready to go meet Pharaoh right now G-d." Now forgive me for this imagination that I'm bringing into this. If that's all the imaginative problems we have Buddy, we would be safe.

All right. So a stick gave him victory in Egypt didn't it? Yeah, defeated the top people of Pharaoh with that stick. Now, in the Wilderness, He was met with another challenge, this time it's from his own people. His people wouldn't have any confidence in his intellectual ability. In his intellectual foresight. And they wouldn't trust his faith that there was a Supreme Being. So, while Moses was away, they got to mumbling and grumbling, and when Moses came back, they were all against each other.

They were attacking each other, with fiery tongues.

And it's called in the Bible (the curse) of fiery tongues. Now, fiery tongues, we know mean, hot headed expressions. Big headed, and hot headed expressions. Same kind of problems black folks have. Everybody want to show off what they know. Don't have any sense hardly at all, but just got to fight, got to resist, got to defy somebody. "Well now, you don't know everything mister". "Can you prove that?" "Where did you get it from?" "Well, mister, you don't have any credentials" "There's no credibility" "You don't have a P.H.D." "You don't have a Masters" "You don't have a Bachelor's Degree" "You don't have anything of substance, Mister!" "So, you're just telling us something with no basis, no proof."

And you say, "well look, you ought to do this on moral grounds. Can't we find a common moral base for agreement" They get hot headed then, because he knows you're going to catch him because he won't stand up morally. He gets hot headed, then he start throwing fiery tongues at you. "You're this, and you're that". "And I would never, if you people follow this sucker, you're going to be disappointed". "I know his game". "In fact, we ought to drive this nigger off the block". "We ought to drive this nigger out of our community". "He isn't nothing but a problem".

So fiery tongues start, right? And then soon as he is about to be established, the next jealous hearted one, say, "well look, you may be right about him, but I'll tell you something, you aren't no good either nigger. I think the best one qualified here to settle this thing and give us some direction is my buddy Joe". Now see, he's going to get out of the focus now because he doesn't want the people to identify him, that he's just attacking because he wants the position. So, He says, "I'm going to put Joe in there first, then I'm going to get it from Joe, because Joe isn't as heavy as me up here." "The one should have it is Joe. He's the most qualified one for it sucker".

So they begin to attack each other with fiery tongues. right? Now, how did Moses deal with that. Moses raised up a Cross in the wilderness. It was a stick, a pole, with a bar across it. He raised up a Cross in the wilderness, and he put a serpent on that Cross, as a symbol. The Cross itself was a symbol, and the serpent itself was another symbol. So he put a serpent, a brazen, or a brass serpent on the Cross, and it appeared as a Crucifix. A serpent crucified on a Cross. Now why did he do that?

44

He did that for the same psychological effect. Remember, He came out of Egypt. The place that had evolved psychology to a very, very high peak. So he knew the psychological benefits of having that Imagery, influenced the emotional behavior of those people. So every time they saw a snake, a snake on the Cross, Crucifix, and they beheld that snake, dead, on that Crucifix, it was a sign that he had interpreted to them (they knew the translation). It was a sign of what their emotional unstableness, and emotional rages had done to their basic constitution.

To their fixed nature. See, human beings had been given a fixed nature hasn't he? And that fixed nature is a nature that opens up, it accepts to be altered, it accepts anything. It accepts to be altered, it accepts to be changed, it accepts to be suppressed, it accepts anything. For the sake of doing what? Releasing the potential in that nature for higher station of life. There's a potential in that nature for a higher development. And that nature will accept to be mistreated. That nature will accept to be altered. That nature will accept to be held down, because nothing can hold back its potential. And pressure is what speeds up its activity to reach its full potential. So it accepts all of that. You see. So Moses, through the symbol, showed his people that when the intellect is heated up too hot, the same thing happens to it, that happens to brass.

Now, we know in ancient symbolism, ancient mythology, the snake is a symbol of fertility. It is a symbol of the creation cycle, survival. The serpent, when it gets cold, he hibernates. When it gets warm, he comes back to action. He comes back into activity. He can survive all kinds of conditions. He has a terribly long age, and many other mysteries about him that we won't go into.

The serpent, without legs, can go up a tree. The serpent without leg's can go across the country. You see. So a serpent without leg's can go horizontal, and can go vertical, without leg's. Now, what is it without leg's that have freedom of movement in all kinds of dimensions. It's our intellect, the human intellect. I can send it up a tree without legs. I can send it into the ground without legs. I can send it across country without legs.

Now, when it becomes a flying Serpent, that means my intellect has broken and unlocked the riddle of the atmosphere. Then it can take wings, (and as the scripture says) and become a flying serpent. Fly the air. Right?. Yes, I hope some of you can follow what I'm saying here. But if you can't follow me in all that I'm saying, the trip is very adventurous isn't it.

So he put the serpent on a pole and raised it up. Showing it dead on the pole. Meaning that intellectual arrogance on your part, intellectual jealousy on your part, will render your mind dead. And he raised that up as a sign to remind his people after he educated them to that particular thing. After educating them to that particular behavior, behavioral risk on the part of their intellect, then he put a sign up there, that held the message in symbol form.

And you know what the Chinese philosopher says. "One picture is worth a thousand words," or did he say ten thousand words? So he raised the symbol up and said, "when any man had that problem, if he just looked on that symbol that Moses raised, He was healed.

Now, don't they tell us, "look on Jesus, and be healed". So here is the value in that symbol that I pointed to in the earlier part of this talk. It's cathartic benefit. It's power to purge the conscience, and to quicken thought and memory, and moral sentiments, to make them stir again in the person. So, what does the book say? The book says, "as the Serpent was raised up in the wilderness, so shall the son of man be lifted up." Isn't that what the book says. What does it mean?

It means, Moses raised the Serpent up, (to speak to a defect in the intellect of his people). Arrogance and emotional rage. Intellectual jealousy. As the Serpent was raised up in the wilderness, so shall the son of man be lifted up. Now, so what does that Jesus mean on the Cross then.

There's a defect in the morals of people. And isn't that where Christianity base itself. That man is created in sin. That this is an inherent, or a natural defect he inherited from Adam, his first father. So they say that we are inherently given to sin. And we need something to redeem us. The thing that redeems us is showing us a guileless person.. A spotless person in terms of sin. Crucified by the world, for no other reason, but for his righteousness.

And that make our sentiments go to him even though we are sinners, and in our sentiments going to him, our being is transferred to his Image, and we become one in Christ, on the Cross. And we begin to recall what Jesus, the new self represents when we're getting involved in crime and immorality. And those that still hold the Image in their conscience will say, "forgive me Lord". Right? "Forgive me Lord." But look, I said in the early part of the talk also, "that a tree is known by the fruit it bears." And we find that wherever the Image has been established, there's the greatness amount of homosexuality, there's a greater amount of behavior perversion's, there's a greater amount of killing, robbing, stealing, and brutalizing and mutilating the flesh of human beings. So, it has an effect of appealing to the conscious of the people and making them feel sorry for that, but it also feeds perversion in the human beings.

Now, if that Image is also feeding perverted behavior in the person, then we must weigh the two together, and look at the benefits. But let me go on to finish this third point. And believe me, it won't be eight hours. I have taught eleven hours, I think once. But it won't be that long. I'm getting old now man, my feet are already hurting, you see. So just be patient, it won't be too much longer. Let us look now at two things here. Two points here. Right now.

One is this. **The Promise in Religion**. What is the promise in religion? Jesus said "I talk to you, or I speak to you in parables now, but however, or howbeit, there will come a time when I will speak to you in plain language". Isn't that the gospel? That's the gospel. So what does that tell me? If the Cross represents a symbolic way of reaching the conscious of people, in order to preserve their moral nature, and moral interest, or moral concerns, then the Bible tells me that there is coming a time when symbols, riddles, parables are going to be pushed back, and out of the way as a veil opening up for the light, and the knowledge shall come to us in plain language that all of us can understand. In other words, that wording in scripture, promises us what America in the West has tried to deliver.

And what is that? Public Education. Equal access to knowledge. And America has pledged right now isn't it? To make college education available to all of its citizens who qualify for it, isn't it? Yes! We have a little dark period right now, because of the certain allowances, certain funds that were available for students are not available now. But, the commitment is still there, and students that qualify are still getting assistance. Aren't they? Yes. Whether they be black, red, or poor.

In fact the poor are the ones that they recognize. So, America is committed to that. And the Bible, if you understand it, if you understand the whole mystery, that's centered, or focused in Jesus, and the Cross, then you understand that the promise is given in that particular New Testament expression, "I speak to you now in parables".

And when someone speaks to you in parables, it's like speaking to you in riddles. It's like speaking to you in concepts that you don't understand. Parables need interpretation. When he says "How be it, the time will come when I will speak to you plainly." Isn't that the New Testament? Well those who understand it, know that this is a promise. The promise that man recognizes as a divine promise, or as divine will, that everybody will one day have the opportunity to see the **Reality of Their Purpose**, their dignity, their destiny, Their potential in this life, in this world.

Now, I won't go into the Islamic view on this particular idea, but I will simply say this, that that was answered in Mohammed (pbuh) because education became an obligation on every male and female, and no one was discriminated against when it came to divine knowledge. In Prophet Mohammed (pbuh), priesthood was abolished, and everybody had equal footing when it came to the opportunity to get the word of G-d, and also the knowledge of that word.

That was established in Prophet Mohammed's (pbuh) time. And over a period of less than fifteen years, he brought what was described as dark age, ignorant masses, warring hoodlum gangs, to be the **Model of Civilization, and Enlightenment for the whole then world**. So that's where we will stop. We will stop there.

You might say, "well, why is your community of Muslims internationally in such a shambles now, Mr. Imam?" Or you might say, "dude, whatever." You may say anything in this nigger situation. You may say anything. The reason for that is because, Jesus Christ was a sign of Prophet Mohammed being Crucified, not as a man, but as the mission. Jesus was a sign of what would come after him. Most of us think that Jesus himself was Crucified. In our Religion, we're told no!, He wasn't Crucified. But is only a sign that really, something was substituted in his place. It's a substitute, it's a transference of your reality to the Image, and you're put into his Image on the Cross. Actually, you, your intellect is Crucified on the Cross, along with the word of G-d. That's Double Cross.

Yes, see when Jesus represent the word of G-d in his physical body, (Double Cross), that is, put on a Cross, Crucified on a Cross, and by you attaching yourself, or putting yourself in the Image, then you have identity in the Image, therefore you, are Crossed, right!. And you are crossed morally, because now, you can't even muster up the moral courage to demand dignity for yourself in the world.

So you are crossed morally. But by the fact that you are crossed morally, and in that Image, you are also crossed intellectually, because without moral life, you will never come into the rational spark. It's impossible. The rational spark comes in the moral body. That's why light illumined in Jesus. Because he was a moral body. That's where the light

illumines. In the moral body. And since you don't have
access to interpretation of the word of G-d, you are cut off
intellectually.

The Promise then, is to bring enlightenment to the world.

So if enlightenment is to come to the world, and Jesus, as a
sign, represent the quickening of moral consciousness that
creates a good situation for the quickening of rational
conscious, then, if he has to go away, what is meant by that?
In the New Testament, he say's "It is expedient that I go
away". He says that, "if I go not away, the comforter will not
come unto you". Now, wasn't he the comforter. But the
scripture also says, another comforter doesn't it? Another
comforter. And G-d will give you another comforter. So
H\he's speaking of that, another comforter. He said, "If I go
not away, the Comforter will not come unto you."

Now, what reconciles human life. What brings it into
harmony? What rests it? What gives it a feeling of
confidence, moral fortitude? But that won't last forever. It's
expedient that that go away. You have to stop depending on
moral light alone. You have to be blessed with insight into

the material composition of the world. In the sciences that
that material composition hold, and the power that it hands
out to the man of science, for raising his life above a moral
bed of consciousness to a rational pike of progress and
productivity. Yes, and isn't that a comforter? Moral life
comforts me until I began to feel the economic bite, and I
say, "Oh lord, thank you for morality, but please take these
terrible economic conditions away, soon" and G-d says, "It's
expedient that you go away, for if you go not away, the
comforter will not come unto you".

So man has to take up his spiritual stake, say, that's enough.
I put my spiritual stake here. This land is declared for
spiritual life. I raise my spiritual flag here. This land's
declared for spiritual life. The principal here, the orientation
here, the theory here, is moral excellence. And he lasts so
long.

And the people say, "we can't stand these material
conditions, something short in your leadership. There's
something lacking in your leadership". Say, "we love you,
you're sweet as can be, but Carter, you got to go". You
weren't ready for that one were you? Well, I know you

weren't ready for that one. But Carter had to go. He had the goodie goodie heart, but he didn't have the vision to take the people rationally, materially, scientifically, out of the situation that America was in.

He had the moral vision, but he was lacking the scientific vision of how to deal with the material and economic and moral, etc. those problems. See, one vision opens up all of them. And when the next one opens up, in order to be successful in it, it has to also be the first one. Therefore, Jesus said, "you don't see me. I go away, and you see me no more, but never the less, you shall see me". Is that right? Meaning that when rational enlightenment) comes, when scientific enlightenment comes, "If I'm not there, G-d didn't do it. And if I'm not there, it won't be successful". Now look at the scientific treasures that this West has come into. But look at the clumsiness, the human clumsiness on their part. They don't look very skilled when we see the history of the movement of America, the west, in human life.

When we look at how human life has suffered, how human life has been abused, how human life has been unjustly suppressed, tormented and polluted, crushed under the weight of a city that wasn't designed with respect for the human need. When we look at all that, we say "yes, they have the technology, but they were clumsy when it came to raising the human edifice". Is that right? So that tell me that they didn't have Jesus. And Jesus said, "I go away. As long as I'm in the world, I am the light of the world". But he said "I have to go away". That tells me that when (Jesus Died), not only did we lose Jesus, The Prophet (pbuh), from this world, but this world that followed him, also lost the light that he brought, because he said, "as long as I'm in the World, I'm the Light of the World".

Now, you will say, "yes, it means that as long as Jesus is in our hearts, the moral light will stay on". I don't think so, because Jesus as you have conceived him, hasn't kept the moral light on. If the moral light was kept on, how come they just discarded us, disregarded us, and wrote us off as an inferior stock, as subhuman people? And then sold us as they sold horses and mules. And treated us worse than they did horses and mules. Used our bodies for their sport on the weekend. Tortured us for sport. Smoked cigars and drank whiskey, and laughed, and enjoyed seeing us tortured, whipped, beat, or put two blacks against each other and let them beat their brains out for forty rounds. You fight ten rounds now, but you fought forty rounds back then. Put two Black's together, and let them fight for forty rounds. Beat each other to death with their fists, for their sport. That means that those people had been deprived of their human intelligence. If this was possible under the Image, then the Image did not have the same effect that Jesus had. That didn't happen in Jesus life did it.

When Jesus was with the people did they treat each other like that. He went along the town, he went along the ways of the town, and he was able to draw people away from cruelties wasn't he? He said, "oh, that suffering man there in the street, don't walk around him, pick him up." Jesus said, "I'll pick him up myself. You won't pick him up, I'll pick him up myself".

He demonstrated what the human being was supposed to do. So if that same concern, if that same power was in America, was in the west, then tell me what brought the West, Europe, and America, to treat human beings as cruelly as they treated us over a period of better than a hundred years and since. Well two hundred years, and then another hundred years of lynching. Jim Crow and lynching. So that tells us that it wasn't there. Now, what is it saying? It's saying that G-d will send you another comforter. "It's expedient that I go away, for if I don't, the Comforter will not come unto you". Prophet Mohammed (pbuh) is the answer of that. Now you all deal with personalities too much. Because that's the way this western culture has conditioned you. That's the way it has orientated your mind and your emotions. You identify too much with physical body, a physical person.

You identify too much with a symbol. You have to be able to identify the meaning that the symbol is nothing but in casing form, or a frame form. Prophet Mohammed, (pbuh) he came and he represents the second comforter. But he also represents the Jesus principal too. He says in the Qur'an, "G-d say's of him, I have lived a whole lifetime with you". And we know his lifetime was forty years. Forty years prior to the coming of the revelation.

Now, what does that forty years symbolize. It symbolizes the moral excellence of Prophet Mohammed (pbuh) before enlightenment dawned in him. G-d missioned him as a Prophet, and taught him. Made him educated. Educated him, and made him the most enlightened person on this earth. Says that G-d, (and the very words of the language, when G-d spoke to Him), tells us that it was an education, or an educated process. He said to Prophet Mohammed, "Read". And Prophet Mohammed said, "I can't read". G-d said it again, He said "Read". Prophet Mohammed said, "I'm not one to Read" He said again. "Prophet Mohammed, He said Read, Oh Mohammed", and Prophet Mohammed began to Read.

Is that in the scripture too? Yes! The scripture says "that there will come a time when there will be a famine, and it won't be a famine of food, it will be a famine of hearing the word of G-d". This is the bible. Say's. "and darkness will engulf the whole world". Wasn't Mohammed (pbuh) born in what they call the dark ages. When darkness engulfed the whole world. Says, "and darkness will engulf the whole world". Says, "and one will come with the word, with the scripture". And they will go to one and they will say, "would you read this for me". And that person will say, "I'm sorry, I can't read this, I'm not a man, or a person of letters".

Meaning that they haven't been educated in the knowledge of how to read the script, the print.   It says, then he would take it to another one, a learned person, and he would say, "would you please read this for me?" This is bible. And that person will say, "sorry, it is sealed." Meaning that it is sealed under symbolic interpretation, and he does not have the insight, he does not have the ability to break the riddle, even though he is Aaron. He cannot break the riddle.

So Allah missioned Prophet Mohammed (pbuh). And He said, "Read Once". "I can't Read". "Read again". "I can't Read". "Read, the third time". He began reading. Then he told him, "o, you wrapped up in your mantle, arise and warn the city". "get up, rise, and warn the city". So he educated him, and then told him to come out of wrappings of the oppressive culture. "o, you and your mantle. Wrapped up in your mantle, rise and warn the city, and go out and teach and enlighten the world." One from among the illiterates given the spark of enlightenment, and then guided by G-d, step by step until it's completion.

Now, this is a miracle isn't it? This is a natural phenomenon. Not only a miracle, this is a natural phenomenon. And in our religion, G-d has shown us this as a natural phenomenon. And that's what Jesus was saying in the new testament when he said, "it's expedient that I go away". Meaning that this thing is created by G-d. It's a behavioral principal of nature. And this dawning of morality, and the dawning of the intellect, inside the moral body, the excellent moral body is a necessity. It is a physical, natural phenomenon, as well as divine will.

So, let us see if we can go a little further now. Let us see now, has that been fulfilled in the crucifix. We go now to the idea of the (last supper). Now, look! In the last supper, who's there in that picture. Twelve men under one. Is that right! Twelve disciples, or apostles under one messenger of G-d. What do they represent. They represent the spiritual kingdom. They represent the sky, the heavens. The sky and the heavens are symbolic of man's spiritual aspirations. So what did Jesus then represent for the people?

He represented a community that promised a new life. (didn't he promise something new). He didn't give it. Not in his day. He said, he prayed, "give us this day, our daily bread". Is that right. And he goes on. "thy kingdom come". Not here.

So he prayed for daily bread. And he prayed for the kingdom. Right. To come down from heaven. Is that right. That it be on earth, as it is in heaven. So his table represented the (heavenly aspirations). When we look at the heavens, what do we see up there. A sign of peace. At night we look at the sky. Oh, it looks so peaceful doesn't it. So quiet and peaceful. So orderly. Things are up there in an orderly arrangement, and they move so orderly, and they're so dependable.

You can clock it and, oh, you came back the same time again, say, "oh sweetheart moon, you came the same time". "baby I thought you'd be a little late tonight". The moon say, "naw, I'm pretty regular". And the sun, you know, at night you get long you know, and you get tired or bored with the night. "oh, I wonder when that sun's coming. I wish it would hurry up". And you get up and you wait. Say, "hey, hey boy. You sure do your own thing don't you. I wanted you a little earlier. You came the same time you did yesterday". The sun say's, "well, I'm pretty regular". Order, peace, regularity, is that right. Isn't that what we want on this earth. Girl kiss you today, kiss you tomorrow, and then two months before she kissed you again.

Say, "hey, what's happening to you girl". Say, "why you kiss me yesterday, and the day before, and the day before, and now, here two weeks has passed, and no kiss?" "You got me used to the kiss. You got me expecting the kiss. You aren't regular. I'm going out and find me a steady". Yeah, isn't that, don't our life call for some kind of system, some kind of systematic order. Some kind of regularity. So man, look at the Heavens as a sign of that. He say, "Oh, I wish it was here. I wish we had that same kind of discipline, that same kind of peace and orderliness, and regularity down here in our community".

So Jesus prayed for that didn't he? He said, "thy kingdom come". So that means Jesus prayed for orderly life, for consistent life, for regular life, to be established on earth. And not only for that, he said, "and the daily bread". The daily bread, he took it and gave it to the poor didn't he. And they charged him with going into the (sacred house), and getting that bread on the Sabbath day. Say, "well that's forbidden". "you did wrong". And Jesus defended it. He quoted past scripture's. (David, right). I think it was David,

and quoted David. He reminded them of David, to justify
what he had done.

Now, what does the daily bread symbolize? Now here again
we have two major concerns being addressed with a symbol.
Bread is a symbol, and we have here two major concerns
being addressed with a symbol. What is the first concern?
The first concern is for the freedom of the human intellect.
And bread, we know is symbolic of doctrine, symbolic of the
teachings of Jesus himself. For the new testament speaks of
people eating bread and compares it with knowledge. And
the new testament speaks of eating meat, and compares it
also with knowledge. This is nothing that we're secretly
disclosing, or any secrets we're exposing. The bible itself
tells you this in plain language. That bread represents
knowledge, and also meat represent's knowledge. So bread
represents a certain kind of knowledge. What kind? How do
they make bread. The bread that we eat today is bread filled
with air, so our bread represents spiritual science.

The bread of the new testament is spiritual science. It's bread
filled with air. Air representing spirit. And we know that
Jesus is called what, "the one blessed with the holy spirit",

and he's called also, "child of the holy spirit". So the doctrine then, or the gospel of Jesus is bread, not meat, bread. And if you study the gospel, he ate bread and fish. Right. He didn't eat any beef. No lamb. And the only thing he had for pork was a curse. This is a fact of the new testament. Some people were possessed by demons. He drove those demons out of those people, into the herd of pigs, and the herd of pigs went crazy and jumped off the cliff and committed suicide.

That's the only connection I know in that bible of Jesus with the pork. That he drove the spirits out of the people that were possessed by them, into a herd of swine. And they became crazy and ran over and jumped over a cliff and committed suicide. Now, I hope you're not one of those swine. And I sure hope you will stop eating them too, but that's beside the point. You don't have to allow that into this discussion today either. Just for emotional effect. If bread then represent spiritual science, you know, the way they make bread now, the bible say's "a certain one put yeast in three measures of bread", is that right. And we know that the Trinitarian doctrine is a doctrine of three. (trinity means three). A certain one put yeast in three measures of bread.

Now, what does the yeast do to the dough? The yeast makes more air get into the dough, and it makes the dough rise. The yeast puts more air into it, and makes it rise. And we know that the new testament doctrine is a highly spiritual doctrine. It's a loaf of bread, raised up very high, with yeast air. Now this is not to criticize. I respect these symbols, and these elements. They hold wisdom, they hold science. In the last supper, let us look and see what was on the table (bread and wine).

Now he said, "do this in remembrance of me." We're still talking about the crucifix. Don't forget our point. We're establishing reasons why that image should go, reasons for its removal. So he said, "do this in remembrance of me." And he broke the bread and he gave it to the disciples, right?

And they all ate of one bread. (meaning they all ate of one doctrine), is that right? And then he also took the wine and they all drank of the same wine (same wine symbolizing that he was telling them to be of the same spirit). And you know now, liquors are called spirits, aren't they? Liquors are called spirits. So one was a spiritual doctrine, and he said, "eat of it." See, the teeth have to work with bread. You don't just swallow bread. You swallow water. You chew bread. See, some kinds of ideas we give you, you don't have to chew it, we say "chew on that awhile". You ever here that expression, "chew on that awhile." It means think about that; ponder on that, think about that for awhile, you see. So, bread represents religious doctrine, or teachings that hold science.

The science for treating the spiritual ill's of the person. And the wine represents the spirit that is connected directly with human sensitivities. And those sensitivities now have become concerns, and we know that concerns are stronger than sensitivities, aren't they. Water represents sensitivities. If you just touch water it quivers all through. Water is very sensitive. But wine represents a higher development in the water. Wine represent concerns. Concerns will stimulate the mind. Concerns, when they are sober concerns, they will stimulate the mind, if they are promising, but they won't necessarily, or they won't drunken the mind. Right?. But we can get concerns that are not understandable, or that are oppressive, or not in accord with the needs of our nature, and those concerns will make us drunk. Won't they? Yes! So that's hard liquor, or the non-communion wine, that's wine that aren't supposed to be taken.

Communion wine is different. Now, if you catch the priest giving the wine around, and it's that 69 wine, don't take it. He's supposed to have water, or grape juice. Water with some red dye in it to symbolize, or to resemble blood, or some red grape juice. That's what he is supposed to have. He isn't supposed to be drinking wine, no real wine. Wine is called the juice of the vine. Now, if you leave it to ferment, it will become something to make you drunk. To intoxicate you. So what is the meaning of this intoxicating effect now. (it means that the people become so emotionally enthused, so emotionally involved into the religion, that the effect on them is the effect of alcohol). And if you increase that too much, you make your congregation drunk, don' you. Yes! That's strong liquor. Strong liquor. Now, no amount of that stuff you buy from the liquor store is justified. G-d forbids that. He says, "surely, alcohol, gambling, and certain other things are work's of the devil. Stay away from them".

But this wine that they take in communion is symbolic of (enthusiastic teaching's). So, Jesus is able to take flat doctrine

that the Jews were dealing out, or giving, and he was able to see insight, and with his insight, he was able to see meaning's in there that they hadn't been able to discover. So, he was able to develop those concepts to a high level, like developing water up to a level of wine. And the people were excited. Like some of you are right now. You perhaps, have listened to religious teachers, or preachers before, but now you're excited.

Your curiosities are excited. Your imagination is excited. So you're like, drinking wine. Like wine, it's exciting for you, it's enthusiastic and everything, so it's like drinking wine. But if I just harp on the moral message, it will be just giving you plain water, and pretty soon, it get's dull, doesn't' it. "oh hell, I'm tired of this nigger telling me I ought to be righteous". "hell, he don't know the rest of the problems I got. I'm going to leave" but there is hardly anyone left here, because it's not flat water, it's a little wine. And you know, wine is hard to resist. You have to have a divine commandant to stay away from it. Especially in the situation of it down here. It throw you into chaos, turmoil, and confusion etc, you know, and everything is going bad, that wine is hard to resist.

You say you have sweet promises. You're sweet tasting. I got to take you. Going back to the last supper. Look at the last supper now. What's offered on the table. Wine and bread. Do you call that a supper? I'm not making fun. There's a sign in this. Do you call that a supper? Haven't you heard of (after dinner wine). (cocktails). (a cocktail, and after dinner wine).

Now, if this was a supper, this tells me that this was, after dinner. Right! It wasn't a cocktail. It didn't say before supper, or brunch, or something like that. This is called supper. So that tells me that this was supper time, and at supper time there was being served at the square table, not the round table, the square table, wine and bread. So that tells me that this was desert. The supper had been finished, and the wine and bread was the desert. That's why they call Jesus "sweet Jesus".

Now, the next time the priest put that cracker on your tongue, if it doesn't taste sweet, tell him, "you're doing all right, but make the bread sweet, because Jesus is (sweet Jesus), and this aren't supper man, this is dessert, after supper, or at supper time". So we know the doctrine of Christianity is

built upon the scientific basis that man is driven helplessly, toward pleasure. Man wants to be pleased. He wants to be happy, and Jesus is given to us as a sweet symbol. He represents everything sweet, nice, and pleasant.

Is that right? Yes! So that's the sweet bread you see, and the wine represents the sweet wine, the sweet spirit in that doctrine. The spirit of what? Love. Love for G-d. Love for your fellow man. Do good, even by your enemies, right. That's the sweet spirit. The spirit of conscience, that motivates you to do good, to be good, in spite of the situation that prompts you, or stimulates you to do wrong, or to do evil, or to be cruel. So here, we have a doctrine, and we have a behavior. We have a doctrine in the bread, and we have a behavior, or a spirit of behavior, in the wine. And that's call the last supper. And I said it's dessert, that came after the supper. It was what he gave them in the end of his life.

During his mission, he gave them instruction. He educated them. And at the end of that mission, there was a supper. He gave them the dessert. And dessert was "to keep the sweet conscience". "to keep the sweet inclinations". "to teach the sweet impulses". "and eat of that, that will sustain that". For what we eat of solids, doesn't it sustain the liquids. Yes. The blood is two things. Nutrients from solids, and liquid from water. Is that right. So there are two. Solids and liquids, that's what it is. Nutrients from solids, and liquids from water. When they come together, they make blood. Now look. If we can only bring the material concerns back into our spiritualism, won't we have blood again. Yes. We need the nutrients of the solids to mix with the water to make blood.

And what does our scripture say. It say's "G-d saw the heavens and the earth separate, and he said, come ye together, willingly or unwillingly". So in scriptural language, he's saying, "that the heavenly aspirations, and the earthly needs have to be reconciled, whether you like it or not". Willingly, or unwillingly. Yes. Let us proceed because this is good. This is a good supper. I bear witness to it. So let's look at the other, see, we said there were two things being addressed by these symbols. So we have just discussed one side.

Prophet Mohammed (pbuh) said, (and those who have studied the Christian sciences, I'm sure that they have been told too), "that the word of G-d addresses two major concerns, and have at least two major and distinct applications". Now, Jesus said, "I come not of water only, but of water and blood". Blood mean's (that particular knowledge that reconcile spirituality with material reality), and water meant (that, that just serves the thirst for moral understanding, relieves the burning in the conscience). Let's look now at the other knowledge that it is addressing. We just mentioned material concerns, and spiritual concerns as the wine, and as the blood.

For Jesus said "take this, (the blood) of the new testament". Right. "take this wine, the blood of the new testament". So now, let us look at the other application, or the other address. It is addressing two more things. Two other things. It is addressing the need for rational life, for intellectual growth, as well as the need for moral growth, and moral life. Water on the other side symbolizes moral life, for we use water to clean ourselves, to clean our garments etc, up until recently. Now, chemicals do the job, and we are filthy as hell. So we have on the other side, water, symbolizing moral life, and bread, symbolizing rational knowledge. And to show you that man has not been deprived completely of that kind of knowledge, you remember us speaking of bread as our rations. And right now in the army, they call it k-rations, right. And k-rations. Rations mean your food.

And it's a play on rational. The rational knowledge. And in the bible you'll find the eating of bread and meat is symbolic of the eating of knowledge, or the digesting of knowledge. The being able to manage knowledge with your intellect, or with your senses, and digest it through the system and grow upon it, right. We restore cells upon it. Dead cells. Put the cells back. It revitalizes. It gives us life again. All of that. Right! Oh yes! You know, in science, they tell us that the skin cells, they undergo a cycle, in 28 to 30 days, they are renewed. And if you have a disease that interrupts that cycle, you will start scaling on the outside. You'll get an ugly looking, terrible looking skin, because that cycle has been hurt, you see. Well, now we're talking about knowledge. And if he said, "eat of my flesh", what was he saying.

On the one side that we have discussed, he was saying, "eat of my material concerns". And on the other side that we are now discussing, he was saying, "eat of my intellectual concerns". We have to get into academic concerns. We have to become educated people. And Jesus didn't represent this to the (ivory tower people), or to the (intellectual's). Jesus was a messenger to the common people, to the whole world, according to the new testament. Is that right.

First to the house of Israel, and then according to the new testament, he missioned his apostles to go out to the whole world. Is that not right. So, and he himself lived among the weak, and the uneducated. So he represented a concern for education, and a concern for material growth, in the poor, oppressed masses, the common people. And Prophet Mohammed (pbuh) acted that out. He was the fulfillment of that sign. For he was a messenger to the illiterate. He's called in the Qur'an, "the um-mi prophet". And his people that he lived among is call the "ummahi". Plural for um-mi. And he addressed them, and he sparked (through the help of G-d), he sparked in them the moral concerns, and he sparked in them, the rational hunger, and they both grew together. And they became the pinnacle, the height, yes, of moral, and rational excellence. Sciences, the interest in science, in the sciences went from there into Europe and sparked (the renaissance), is that right.

This is history. This is what western scholars say. And also ethics was quickened. The love for ethics was quickened again, was sparked again. And the society's of the world became more ethical. Their cultures became clean, more civilized, more human. So dear beloved people, look at this. This is saying that Jesus promised something. "thy kingdom come, thy will be done. Give us this day, our daily bread".

He promised something, and these things, these symbols in the last supper, promises us that the poor, the oppressed people will have material freedom. They will have free access to higher education. They will have moral based life, ethics, and they will have also, the material conveniences, education, material conveniences. Doesn't one open up the other. Material concerns, brings us into material involvement. Material involvement brings us into the rational understanding of the material basis. The material nature, the sciences etc. They go hand and hand. Material and education. Spirituality and morality. Don't they go hand and hand. Spirituality and morality, material goods and education. So this is the promise dear people.

Now, has that sign fulfilled that promise. Has it (crucified man on the cross), fulfilled that promise. I can prove to you with just a minute or so, (because most of you are almost as old as I am), and a man told me on the plane, he said, "well, you're going downhill". I said, "we don't have long to go".

"I said (we) don't have long to go". Again, that was beside the point too. He was trying to be funny with me. I put it right back on him. And he was about my age. He might have been younger, but he looked like he was in worse shape than I am. And I guess he saw all the white hair in my beard, and my bald head, he said "yeah, you're going over the hill". I said, "yes, we don't have long to go". So dear beloved people, concluding this third reason for us getting rid of it, we say that the (crucifix), has not promoted these concerns.

Everywhere the crucifix has gone, and everywhere it has been established, there have been the confusion of the social life of the people, the vision of the people, social turmoil, in most places racism. This is a fact. Nothing but a fact. Racial cruelties etc. And also, along with that, has been a tendency on the part of the people who have really emerged themselves, or have been submerged in that idea, to neglect the essentials of life. They are lazy, not responsible, not civic responsible, not to speak of being economically, materially responsible people. Their communities are the most materially neglected. I'm talking about the masses that absorb themselves in that particular (crucifix symbol). And also, cruelty toward each other. So, if it hasn't been able to deliver what Jesus represent, and what he promise in his own symbol, then what good has it been. It hasn't been much good at all. Now, I would like to tell you one more thing before going to the fourth. We're really holding you a long time. I'm going to try to beat the sun down. It's not quite dark. I still see daylight in the window.

Now, look. When Jesus was on the cross, (in the new testament), and I'm saying this, (my people will tell you I do this all the time). This is no special occasion. This is the way I talk all the time. Whatever I have, I give it to whoever is present. And it is my hope that it will reach people that are in responsible positions of leadership for the ghetto, for the masses, for the oppressed masses, and that they will catch on to this, and not in my name, but in the name of whatever they believe in, share what they're getting. That's my only hope, that they will take what we're talking about, and have the courage to do what we're doing. That is, have the courage to do what Jesus is supposedly have done and cost him his life on earth. Have the courage to upset the high peoples monopoly on the treasures of life. They are not entitled to that monopoly, and we should upset that. Now, oh yes, getting back to the last point here.

The new testament tells us, that when Jesus was put on the cross, it was the ninth hour, and he supposedly died in the eleventh hour, and this is not, again, this is not to make mockery. In fact, none of you should be offended by what I'm saying. My brother reverend, you should not be offended by what I'm saying because it's not me, it's the "gospel speaking", and my concern is not to injure you, or take anything from you, but to compliment everybody, or to share. Now, it says, "that on the eleventh hour, that he died", and we know the church began its service in the eleventh hour.

Now we know, they say, "well that that means that we base our hope in Jesus, who gave his life that we may live". So it was the act of giving himself, his own life, that makes it possible for us to live. We began living when Jesus died, or we began living at his time of death. So that's the eleventh hour. We know that, but let's look at something else. The new testament say's, "that Jesus, on the cross, thirsted", and we know that Jesus hungered and thirsted, didn't he. He said, "I was a hunger, and you didn't feed me, but I know they said, "oh, he was talking about his followers". He didn't hunger, but he was talking about his followers. So when he ate bread, he was eating bread, demonstrating what his followers needed, and when he drank wine, he was demonstrating what his followers needed. So when he went up upon the cross, he was demonstrating what was going to happen to his followers, and when he died, he was demonstrating what was going to happen to his followers". So if we started at one place, we have to continue it, in other words, none of that stuff happened to him at all. Ok, let's go back now.

Say's, in the eleventh hour, Jesus thirsted (or around that time), and they brought him something. They brought him vinegar and hyssop. A herb and some vinegar. Now, what is another term for vinegar. Vinegar is acid. And another term for vinegar in Italian and Spanish is (acita). Now, if you want to use a descriptive word to describe something that has a vinegar taste, you would say, it is (acetic). Now, this word

(acetic), is a play on (ascetic), and it directs the scholar to (asceticism.) When Jesus passed, who succeeded him as authority on earth. It was the Catholicism. The pope, and Catholicism. And what does their order represent, "asceticism". Asceticism for the order, for the hierarchy of the church. Asceticism, right. So asceticism is (what killed him). It says, "and when he took that, right away he gave up the ghost". It mean, he gave up the (holy ghost). Not just life, he gave up the ghost. And he was born of the ghost. He was born of the holy ghost. It said, "at that point, he gave up the ghost". It didn't say (holy ghost), because he didn't want to tell you too much. Only the sharp witted, the G-d guided people, they would know that it meant, (he gave up the holy ghost).

And it doesn't mean he gave up the holy ghost, it means his order, his people, his followers gave up the holy ghost. The holy ghost left them. And instead of having the holy ghost, that is, the spirit that lead them to the life of the comforter, (the second comforter, rational enlightenment), instead of having that spirit of inspiration in them, they were devoid of it. Asceticism killed that aspiration in them. Yes. So now dear people, if the cross represents that, then why should they say that's the (son of G-d) on that cross. Why don't they tell the truth, and say that's a symbol of humanity on that cross, and then I could go along with the church leaders who have suggested to me an alternative. They say, "look, can't we make a compromise Imam?"

They say, "we don't have any problems. Let everybody put the image in their own image. Let it be Chinese for Chinese, Jewish for Jews, white for the white folks, black for the black folks". That's the way they want to dismiss the problem, that every man is to (see Jesus in his own image). If that's a fact, then let's tell every man that that's not
"G-d on that cross".

Now, number four, lastly. We're finally at the last point we want to establish today for the removal of the crucifix. And you see, I'm closing up the paper so that means we might beat the sun down.

Now, the last point is this. In the study of symbolism, and how it moves, and is correlated or intertwined with man's cultural development, and when we see in anthropology, especially where anthropology addresses the cultural development, the cultural growth of man. We find that man has strained and struggled to bring communication, rational, intellectual idea's to put them into language that will articulate those idea's for him, and to bring his thoughts, his idea's, plainly to any man. When he doesn't have to take a man and put him in a special school and train him in the knowledge of symbolism etc., and then begin to educate him. That he could take a man straight from the street and right away begin to address him and educate him.

This has been the burden on intelligent communication. And man has had to take concrete symbols, and establish them as concepts by which he communicated with his fellow man. Now, we go and we look at another movement, and this movement is the movement of symbolism, as it is found in religion. Man has had a need to see his idea's in himself, and not only himself, but he found a need to capsulize the information that an object held, or a force held, or a principle held.

If he wanted to talk about electricity, he would put electricity in human image and he would call it the G-d Electra. The people who progressed the most in this kind of idea were the

Greeks, the people of ancient Greece. They had a whole pantheon of G-d's. Many G-d's. And these G-d's were in human imaginative form. Not real form, but they imagined them as human beings in human form. So Electra was a G-d. Zeus was a G-d who was over all the others. He was over all the other G-d's. Apollo was a G-d. Apollo was a G-d symbolizing the main motivation, or the main generative force in creation. It was symbolized also as the sun. But Apollo, he was the one who drove the sun. "say, how could he drive the sun".

Well, in this picture of this idea of this wisdom, Apollo had four horses. Four black horses, and a carriage. And the carriage carried the sun, and the horses pulled the carriage, and he (Apollo), steered it. Right. This is in mythology. Greek mythology. So we find that man has had to rely upon human concepts in order to attract human interest. Human beings are automatically easily attracted to an image of themselves. As we have heard, likeness attracts. You recall that. Now, you know what it was now! I know what I'm saying, and you know what it was. Likeness attracts. So man is attracted to his own image. So he get's curious. He's self curious. Isn't that a fact, that human beings is self curious.

The thing that occupy him most is himself. He want to know why. What is this. But the culture can be orientated in such a way that it will take us from this central concern, and attach our concerns to just frivolous kinds of interests. So man had to pick up concretes, and the last concrete he picked up (because Greece was a very, very evolved culture, the Grecian culture, very evolved culture), they had the sciences, they had the divisions of labor, they had highly developed culture. They had everything. Don't think the past is inferior.

The past is superior to most of the communities on this earth. That's a fact of history. Ok, you say, "well did they have airplanes back there"?. Man, that's not the measure of progress. So man picked up different objects in his environment as a symbol to attract the conscious, or the mind of the intellectual interest so that that symbol then will begin to represent, and radiate, or express other disciplines of knowledge to the society or to the person through the medium of that symbol. So the human being was the last thing he stopped upon. That was the last thing he erected, the human being. That was a long time ago. Long time ago. Now, why is there no more need. Is there a need for this? That's the utility. Again, that's a utility, right. But is there still a need for this. No. Why do we have to say that this is deity. How come this started in the first place. History tells us, science tells us, that it started in the first place because man was superstitious. Even the Grecian society was superstitious.

With all of their science, (they were developed quite well), but they were superstitious too. They believed that certain phenomena in the external world held bad Oman's for them, right. And because they didn't have, a truly enlightened mind, (they had been introduced to materialism, and the material sciences) but they hadn't been introduced into the human sciences, and because they didn't have that kind of enlightenment, when the materialism grew, it toppled the establishment.

The Greeks gave themselves to material luxuries, to material comforts, to material extravagance, and they lost their interest in the sciences. They lost their interest in building up a culture, and they collapsed, because of that. Right. One of the nations that fell is call Pompeii. The destruction of Pompeii. You heard about that. Now, the word pompous, come from Pompeii, and pompous mean's giving too much to extravagance, as it relates to luxuries, right. They call it pompous. You go in a man's house and he got mink on his couch. He just got out of his rolls royce. There was mink on the dash board of his rolls royce, and you go in his house and there is mink on the mantle there, and rugs running upside the wall, and jewelry and sparkles all over the place, and you say, "this guy is very pompous". Pomp and glitter. Right, pomp and glitter.

So we understand then that man depended upon those concretes because he had not become yet, free, in terms of the need for him to understand himself, his own nature, himself, his own reality. So man put himself up as an image, as a symbol, because he didn't know his own reality.

Allah say's in the Qur'an, "the creation of this universe is a bigger creation than yours". It tells us that the universal scheme is bigger than man. So don't raise your own image up, thinking your image is the perfect, and it hold's everything. No! You're smaller than the creation. So if we would put the universe, the galaxies on the cross, it would be a bigger interest, a bigger significance. "oh no!,

G-d's son is bigger than the whole creation". That's not what our scripture say's. Our scripture say's "G-d's servant is what is meant in the expression G-d's son". And it says that, "none, no creature, nothing can come to him, angel, or man, or jinn. Nothing can come to him, except as a servant". "that he can't be approached by no equals". He has no equal, and if you understand the new testament, it says, "the sent is not equal to the sender".

And many other things I can quote for another half hour to substantiate that. So, dear beloved people, in our last point we're saying that the evolution of this particular need, the progress of this need in expression in the human intellect for rational, clear, articulate expression, stopped with the human concept, or the human symbol, because man had not yet been introduced into the human sciences. He was just struggling and searching. The Greek's were struggling and searching to understand the sciences of the human nature and the human spirit, and they had not come into the full grasp of those sciences, therefore they tolerated those images, and today, our masses are still burdened by an image on the cross, a symbol that is called (in Christianity) a mystery. The cross is called the mystery. Jesus Christ (pbuh) is called a mystery, and his mother (may G-d be pleased with her) is also called a mystery. All of these things are called a mystery.

So why should we be burdened with all these mysteries, now that science has dawned in the world, and the common man has access to science. And we have schools of higher learning that welcome the common man, and our government has made it a law that the common man must have access to those schools of higher learning. Then, doesn't it go counter to our interests, and isn't it out of step with the time of man, the masses growth and development. Isn't it out of step with them to still go back and depend on those primitive, savage, barbaric kind's of concept's, in order to attract man to human, to morals, and to community

Concerns. It's time to put it down. Please help us. For your own sake, as well as for the sake of all of us, help us advance this particular committee, and it's efforts (to remove all images that claim to represent, depict, or portray the divine).

Peace be unto you. Thank you for your patience. Good to
see all of you here. A lot of you have come a long way's.
You've driven for two or three days. Allah bless you, and if
you have faith like I do, you know that today was a blessing.
Today was a blessing from heaven. This is Dallas Texas.
About a year or so ago, they had a hundred and seventeen
degree's in this town. In this month, I think it was august. I
remember myself, hearing a report it was a hundred and
eleven degree's. And Allah made it cool for us today. The
sky was cloudy so the sun didn't beat down on us. The walk
you made, was in the shade. I came out, it felt so nice. I
think I want to make my home Dallas. I don't think that I can
do it, but I don't want to go back to Chicago. I can't think of,
oh, I don't want to think of what happens in Chicago during
the winter.

This is a very beautiful city. I said in my talk Friday, at the
Judah, "that this city equal's, and maybe it even surpass
Chicago in beauty, skyline, and also down here". Very
beautiful city.

So let us thank Allah for this Meeting, and for the Peace, and for the Conveniences, and for the mild weather, considering what it could be in Dallas in August. Let us thank Allah for all of that, and let us make it our business, and right now begin to thirst and hunger for another meeting of this type. At least once a year we want to invite people from around the country to come and demonstrate their support for One Major Concern. Peace be unto You. As-Salaam-Alaikum.

TAKBIR! TAKBIR! TAKBIR! TAKBIR! Allah-U-Akbar.

ABOUT THE AUTHOR

Imam W. Deen Mohammed was unanimously elected as leader of his community after the passing of his father in 1975; the Honorable Elijah Muhammad, founder, leader, and builder of the Nation of Islam.

At a very early age, Imam Mohammed developed a keen scholastic interest in science, psychology and religion. He began his education, from elementary through secondary school, at the University of Islam in Chicago. Further educational pursuits took him to Wilson Junior College, where he concentrated on microbiology and to the Loop Junior College where he studied English, history, and the social sciences. However, his primary education has come from, and through, his continued pursuit of religion and social truths.

Imam Mohammed's astute leadership, profound social commentary on major issues, piercing scriptural insight into the Torah, Bible and Qur'an, and his unique ability to apply scriptural interpretation to social issues have brought him numerous awards and high honors. He is a man of vision who has performed many historical 'firsts'.

In 1992, he delivered the first invocation in the U.S. senate to be given by a Muslim. In 1993 he gave an Islamic prayer at President William Jefferson Clinton's first inaugural interfaith prayer service, and again in 1997 at President Clinton's second inaugural interfaith prayer service. His strong interest in interfaith dialogue led him to address the Muslim-Jewish conference on March 6, 1995, with leaders of Islam and reform Judaism in Glencoe, IL. In October of 1996, Imam Mohammed met Pope John Paul, II, at the Vatican, at the invitation of Archbishop William Cardinal Keeler and the Focolare Movement. He met with the Pope again, on October 28, 1999, on the "Eve of the New Millennium" in St. Peter's basilica with many other world-religious leaders.

In 1997, the Focolare Movement presented him with the "Luminosa Award", for promoting interfaith dialogue, peace, and understanding in the U.S.

In 1999, Imam Mohammed served on the advisory panel for Religious Freedom Abroad, formed by Secretary of State Madeline Albright. He assisted in promoting religious freedom in the United States and abroad.

In April, 2005, Imam Mohammed participated in a program that featured, "a conversation with Imam W. Deen Mohammed and Cardinal George of the Catholic Archdiocese."

There are many more accolades, achievements and accomplishments made by Imam W. Deen Mohammed. His honorary Doctorates, Mayoral, and Gubernatorial Proclamations give testament to his recognized voice, and the benefit of his leadership to Muslims and non-Muslims alike. He was appointed to the World Supreme Council of Mosques because of the value of his work and leadership in America.

Today, the dignity and world recognition Imam Mohammed has generated is seen all across the world.

Purchase Copies Of This Publication:

WDM Publications
PO Box 1944, Calumet City, IL 60409

Phone: 708-862-7733
Email: wdmpublications@sbcglobal.net

www.WDMPublications.com

For More On Imam W. Deen Mohammed

The Ministry of Imam W. Deen Mohammed
PO Box 1061, Calumet City, IL 60409

Phone: 708-679-1587
Email: wdmministry@sbcglobal.net

www.TheMosqueCares.com

Made in the USA
Charleston, SC
03 February 2013